GW00671149

GLORIOUS HAMPSHIRE

The Beautiful and Varied Landscapes of a Very English County

COLIN ROBERTS

HALSGROVE

First published in Great Britain in 2014

British Library Cataloguing-in-Publication Data
A CIP record for this title is available from the British Library

ISBN 978 0 85704 250 7

HALSGROVE
Halsgrove House,
Ryelands Business Park,
Bagley Road, Wellington, Somerset TA21 9PZ
Tel: 01823 653777 Fax: 01823 216796
email: sales@halsgrove.com

Part of the Halsgrove group of companies
Information on all Halsgrove titles is available at: www.halsgrove.com

Printed in China by Everbest Printing Co Ltd

For my family

CONTENTS

A remote beech tree on the Hampshire Downs

INTRODUCTION

When I took up landscape photography I was soon drawn to the north and west of Britain – to areas of wilderness, mountains and rugged coast. In such places beauty and drama are undisguised, self-evident and even conspicuous. Elsewhere these qualities are more elusive and perhaps more subtle, but are no less inspiring where they are found.

For thirty years I've wandered through rural Hampshire, my county home since childhood, and witnessed some of the finest sights I could have hoped for. Many of my favourite images come from this part of England where the downs, forests and chalk streams form a landscape with a quality of its own.

Few of my photographs are spontaneous; instead they are usually planned – days or even months in advance. My approach is to explore an area and reflect upon it, and only then begin to envisage how I would portray it. I think of light and atmosphere, and how I might use them to bring an intensity to the scene. I also consider extreme weather like snow, frost or fog and how its effects could enhance the subject. With these impressions in mind I return – when the time is right – to work on the photograph. By this slow process I hope to produce something which gives a deeper 'sense of place'.

The beauty of working in Hampshire is that I'm able to apply this planned approach without the restrictions that are inevitable when I'm further from home. What's more, as time passes my style evolves and I can return to locations with new ideas.

Apart from the day-to-day changes in weather, it is the seasons which guide most of my work. Spring is a time for woodland flowers and trees coming into leaf, while in summer I'm drawn to the grasslands, moors and fields. In autumn it is back to the woods or to the downs for the morning mist, while winter is a time for the open landscape and the stark beauty of leafless trees. Following this cycle, I've divided the book into four chapters, allocating each image to the season which it portrays.

The images in this book represent my visual highlights of Hampshire's landscape.

Pines in the mist, New Forest

Landscape at Longstock
A footpath which leads northwards from Longstock gives a striking view across the wooded valley of the Test towards Leckford. The path makes a fine early morning walk, especially in clear weather when the sun can be seen rising beyond the river to the east. I once took this route in late summer and found the fields knee-deep in clover, planted as a crop but looking magnificent with its rosy-pink blooms soaked in dew.

Sunrise from the footpath at Longstock

The photograph on this page shows the view from the path in early spring, when the fields were beginning to turn green. I was drawn to make this particular composition by the two arching walnut trees and the sweeping line of the landscape.

Lime Tree Avenue at Woodmancott
Leading from Woodmancott church up to College Wood is an avenue of young lime trees planted alongside the footpath. Numbering forty-four and with trunks that are clean from the ground up, they have none of the untidy-looking sprouts which are so often seen at the bases of mature limes.

Some years ago I photographed these trees in snow when they were little more than saplings, but more recently I visited on a misty morning in early May. The trees looked splendid in the dawn light, and their emerging foliage helped to soften the scene, which might otherwise have been a rather stark view of woody architecture. Avenues of trees are a recurring theme in my work, and I'm fascinated by the way in which they draw the eye into the scene.

Spring at Woodmancott

Wild cherry blossom on the lane to Ashley

Blossom near Ashley

In spring and summer when the countryside is flushed with wildflowers it's easy to forget the contribution being made by trees. Among others blackthorn, hawthorn, wild cherry, willow and chestnut all add to the floral beauty in the landscape.

I was reminded of this when I came across some cherry blossom near Farley Mount in mid-April. The tree stands in the hedgerow beside the lane on Ashley Down against the backdrop of a wide sloping field. A number of yews on its western side must provide something of a windbreak, helping to shield its delicate blossoms from the prevailing wind. The petals shone brilliant white in the spring sunlight, making a vivid contrast with the rustic bark and green field beyond.

Bluebells at Micheldever Forest

As one who follows nature, it's my belief that few sights can be more inspiring than a deciduous woodland coming into leaf. At Micheldever the display is taken to an extreme, with beech trees and bluebells dominating the scene. The tapering boughs of pale green leaves arching over a fragrant blue carpet create a natural spectacle year after year.

When I'm working in woodlands I prefer the soft light of overcast days – it avoids the harsh shadows created by bright sunlight, and reveals details more clearly. When this photograph was taken an unseasonal mist gave a shadowless light, and softened the vibrant colours to give a more atmospheric scene.

At Micheldever in April

Stitchwort, bluebells and Solomon's seal in Harewood

Wildflowers at Harewood Forest

A short distance from Andover Down is an area of native woodland, dense with oak and hazel. Part of Harewood Forest, it looks lovely in spring when wildflowers create a mottled carpet in their rush to bloom before the canopy thickens.

I went to the wood in late April, taking a footpath which leads in from the north. The route cuts through dense patches of dog's mercury before twisting its way passt mossy boles and scatterings of bluebells. Further in I found clusters of stitchwort – pure white stars on thread-like stems which stood out against the harmonious mix of blue and green.

Embley Wood

Embley Wood is a beech plantation which borders the motorway near East Stratton, and despite the constant hum of traffic there are some fine displays of bluebells in spring. A track leading from the Lane provides the best route into the woods which lie on a partly sloping site. The best areas of bluebells are to the left of the track, where the remains of a small hut stand – a curious dark-framed structure which looks at odds with its lush surroundings. From some angles it's possible to look right through its hollow interior to the woodland beyond.

But away from this forbidding feature the bluebells look magnificent, extending in vast drifts like those at Rownest and Micheldever. In this photograph I opted for a viewpoint which showed the lines of a track converging towards the top-centre of the image.

Bluebells at Embley Wood

Beaulieu Heath

The heaths of the New Forest would not be the same without the occasional scattering of Scots pines. These native conifers make natural focal points in the open landscape, with their vertical structures breaking the monotony of the horizon.

I've paid many visits to Beaulieu Heath where a cluster of three pines stand on a small ridge, forming a strong natural composition against the dawn sky. This photograph was taken in late March when a morning mist engulfed the surrounding landscape.

Pines in the dawn light on Beaulieu Heath

Waggoner's Wells

A list of Hampshire's most tranquil spots would have to include Waggoner's Wells. A string of small lakes on the county's eastern border near Grayshott, they are approached by a quiet lane, edged with ferns, which descends deep into a wooded valley. A small stream connects the lakes which are hemmed in by beech trees and partly lined with rushes. There are plenty of leafy footpaths, and although the lakes are only a short distance apart, each one is seen in isolation because the woodland canopy between them is so dense.

For the photographer Waggoner's Wells is a place of dappled light and reflections – the sheltered location means the waters rarely show much of a ripple. The low-slung boughs of beech trees dip right out over the water, and in spring when they come into leaf the lakes shimmer with pale green. In autumn the waters are thick with fallen leaves and the woods are transformed to a mosaic of orange and brown. When winter arrives and the canopy is gone, the woods are for once light and airy, and the waters reflect the twisting outlines of the leafless trees.

A placid woodland pool at Waggoner's Wells

Ramsons in Fulley Wood

Fulley Wood near Tichborne

Fulley Wood is a peaceful stretch of native woodland between Tichborne and Gander Down. It abounds with wildflowers in spring – Solomon's seal, bluebells and ramsons (wild garlic) stretch in deep beds beneath the arches of hazel.

A footpath enters the wood from the lane near Ovington Down Farm and then runs alongside the trees before dipping away across the field to Tichborne. The air was heavy with the scent of wildflowers when I walked this way on a damp day in late April, and as I approached an area of ramsons I noticed a cluster of fresh beech leaves growing from a stump, making an unusual focal point among the flowers.

Trees at Hinton Ampner
Many deciduous trees have a stark beauty in their leafless form. Indeed, mature specimens growing in open places can offer more to the eye in winter through their woody outline than they do when cloaked in summer foliage.

This oak at Hinton Ampner, which has a marked southward lean, is no veteran but is developing a rugged appearance which is characteristic of the species. This is in contrast to the distant lime trees which are younger, taller and more rounded in profile.

Oak and lime in the parkland at Hinton Ampner

Longstock's thatched river hut in late May

Thatched hut at Longstock

Although I'm normally drawn to wilder places without man-made features, this location in the central Test Valley has always been an exception. The small thatched hut perched on an island in mid-river complements the scene, its very fabric echoing the reeds and willows in the landscape beyond. The trout-shaped weather vane then adds to the narrative, being symbolic of the role which the river has played for man over the centuries. For photographers it's an idyllic scene which never loses its appeal.

Side-lit beech trees at Broughton Down

Broughton Down

Approaching Broughton Down from the south is a byway which is edged on one side with beech trees, their trunks packed tightly together in a regimented line which runs for half a mile. It seems likely to me that the trees were originally planted as a hedge, but were then allowed to grow unchecked into maturity, so that they now arch gracefully over the track. Their line is unbroken except for a small gap at the southern end which – I remember – was cut around 1990 when an underground pipeline was being laid.

The trees look particularly impressive when their trunks are side-lit by the morning sun. This photograph shows the view looking southwards down the byway, and was taken shortly after sunrise in late March.

Black Wood

Although not a natural feature, the beech plantations of Hampshire have been an integral part of the landscape for generations. And while the shade they cast inhibits the undergrowth to an extent, early spring flowers thrive on the leafy woodland floor before the canopy advances. Black Wood near Popham is one of the largest, and though many people pass it (it's bordered to the north by the busy A303), few stop to enjoy it – I've seen only a handful of walkers during my many visits.

A convenient route into the wood is from Larkwhistle Farm Road where a gravel track enters the southern section. It passes through an area of mixed trees and leads towards the centre where there is a small patch of open land. The pure stands of beech are to the north and are criss-crossed by a number of paths. This photograph was taken in late April when the newly-unfolded beech leaves were still soft and translucent.

Beech leaves in spring at Black Wood

The wild, towering beech trees in High Croft Wood

High Croft Wood

I came across High Croft Wood while horse-riding with my wife in the New Forest a number of years ago, and remembered it as an enchanting place. An ancient track tunnels its way into the woods, banked by a knotted framework of exposed roots put down by beech trees in their struggle to grip the unstable ground. The root systems are thick with moss and lichen, and the towering trunks look statuesque as they reach for the canopy.

My first thoughts were to photograph the scene in autumn, but when I returned in November I found that the newly-fallen leaves masked the mossy roots and the scene looked slightly sombre. So I made a further visit in early May of the following year and found conditions much more favourable, with a subtle green light filtering through the young foliage.

Spring in the beechwoods at Upper Canterton

Upper Canterton

Near the hamlet of Upper Canterton in the New Forest there is an area of deciduous trees dominated by beech. The uncluttered woodland floor is cloaked in their orange-brown leaves, and for a few weeks each spring there is a remarkable contrast between the pale green foliage above and that which is underfoot.

As it happens the site is only a couple of hundred yards from the busy A31 trunk road, which borders the wood to the south. But surprisingly this detracts little from the beauty of the place – the dip of the land and the sound barrier created by the trees means that the road noise is negligible.

Ocknell Pond

The disused Second World War airfield at Stony Cross in the New Forest is a peaceful place today. The runway once used by Hurricane fighters is now a quiet road frequented as much by wandering ponies as it is by cars.

I found the place quieter still when I arrived on a foggy morning in January, heading for the remote Ocknell Pond on the west side of the plain. Surrounded by gorse, and sometimes hard to locate, the pond was swollen on this occasion by heavy winter rains. As I made my way along the water's edge and weighed up different compositions the air began to clear and cloud-forms became visible above the fog. I settled for a view looking south towards Fritham Cross where the slanting rays of early sunlight cut across the scene.

Reflections at Ocknell Pond

One of the lonely field oaks at Chilton Candover

Lime Tree Avenue near Oakley

A small lane which leads northwards from Oakley is edged with lime trees, tall mature specimens which must date from the nineteenth century. But they are not set back from the lane, or widely spaced like the usual avenue plantings found in parkland. Instead they stand within touching distance of the road and jostle closely together at no more than a few yards apart, making the lane feel more like a passageway or wooded tunnel.

I passed this way one day in May, having come to see the trees in their spring foliage. The early sun was dispersing the morning mist, and it soon became bright enough to cast a soft sidelight across the lane, illuminating the freshly-emerged heart-shaped leaves.

The lane between the lime trees near Oakley

Barnet Side

The quiet country lanes between East Tisted and High Cross – an area known as Barnet Side – are a haven for wildflowers. In early May every hedgerow is thick with bluebells, stitchwort, cow parsley and buttercups, while above them hang heavy blossoms of hawthorn and prickly strands of budding bramble.

Among this busy display are patches of the more subtle Solomon's seal, with its unusual arching fronds. To my eye it's a distinguished looking plant, and one of my favourite spring flowers, for although its white bell-like flowers are small, its graceful shape sets it apart from its more flashy companions.

Solomon's seal in the hedgerow near Claypit Farm

Dandelion clocks near Hermitage Farm

Beyond the thickening hedges some of the fields are full of dandelions, most of which have gone to seed by mid-May. When exploring the area I once took a footpath near Hermitage Farm and found a swathe of dandelion clocks in the shelter of a hedge, untouched by the wind.

Roman Road near Bossington
Using a detailed map it's possible to trace the course of a Roman road which heads west from Winchester and leads to Old Sarum at Salisbury in Wiltshire. In physical terms much of the route has vanished beneath fields and is no longer even used as a path, but by my reckoning around 8 miles of country lanes still follow the way set by the Romans. This photograph shows one stretch at Broughton Hill, a mile or so west of Bossington, where it passes through an area of tranquil woodland.

Strangely, the main Winchester to Salisbury route of today uses none of the Roman road, but instead follows an arc to the north which is several miles longer.

The Roman road near Bossington – now a wooded lane

A misty morning by Cadnam cricket green

Birch Trees at Cadnam

For a tree of only modest size the silver birch makes a considerable contribution to the New Forest landscape. It is found in the woods, on the heaths, along roadsides and stream-banks, and in all these places its presence is emphasized by its shining bark. But to my eyes the most attractive feature of this native tree is its graceful aspect, which is seen most clearly against a morning mist.

Cadnam cricket green is surrounded by a grassy common dotted with birch trees, and I visited the place early one morning to photograph them. I noticed a particular clump whose trunks appeared to lean together in harmony, with their feathery foliage hanging motionless in the damp air.

SUMMER

Rosebay Willowherb on the North Wessex Downs
Hidden away in the upper reaches of the North Wessex Downs, I came across a hillside cloaked in rosebay willowherb. The tall pink-purple flowers were visible from afar, but it was only at close quarters that the real beauty of the slender blooms could be seen.

I wanted to capture an image which conveyed a sense of depth, so I walked up the slope to a position where I could see the wide swathe of flowers dipping away to the woodland beyond. From this angle I was also able to eliminate the sky and create a more simple composition dominated by trees and flowers alone.

Drifts of rosebay willowherb on a slope of the North Wessex Downs

River Itchen at Ovington

Located at the centre of my county map is the upper Itchen Valley, where this tranquil scene was photographed. It shows a wooden footbridge which spans the river at Ovington and was taken in midsummer shortly after sunrise. It's an attractive place in any season, but I chose to portray it in June when the surrounding landscape has an almost luxuriant feel. The banks are thick with reeds and rushes, and the distant trees – willow and ash among them – are in full leaf, and all this creates a mosaic of green foliage which is reflected in the water below.

To me it seems fitting that a view which captures the essence of rural Hampshire should be found in the very heart of the county.

The peaceful waters of the Itchen at Ovington

Cow parsley by a barley field at Sparsholt

Rolling Fields at Sparsholt

There are some splendid walks around Sparsholt, a small village set in the gently sculptured landscape west of Winchester. I've ventured this way a number of times in May and June when the countryside is flushed with a new season's growth, admiring the sweeping fields and looking for wildflowers in the hedgerows.

As in many places, cow parsley dominates – occasionally growing so deep and dense that no other plants are visible. Being so commonplace, the beauty of this plant is often overlooked, but I've no doubt that if the lanes and byways were not lined with its bright white flowers it would soon be missed. As a child I came to know it for its dried hollow stems – sometimes four feet long – which were a regular hedgerow feature on winter walks near Winchester.

The image of cow parsley was taken in early June, where the flowers were reaching out from the hedge towards the rolling fields of young barley. Nearby on the same morning I noticed a young fallow deer picking its way through the field – it looked up and watched intently before taking fright and bounding away.

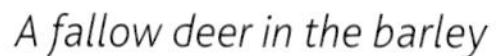

A fallow deer in the barley

Gander Down

Four miles east of Winchester the South Downs Way passes a remote oak – a stout specimen which mushrooms up in the middle of a vast field. The path then continues across the lane and over the broad shoulder of Gander Down, passing a tumulus on its way. At sunrise the down makes an inspiring scene, but it's also a place with a sad event in its distant past. A memorial at Tichborne church 2 miles to the north tells how Richard Tichborne, the infant son of a baronet, drowned in a cart rut on the down in 1619.

Ash with oak on Gander Down

I have a map of the area dated 1963 which shows that a small copse adjoined the lane and extended up across the down, but this has since been cleared, leaving only a scattering of oak and ash which themselves have become depleted in recent years. The image shows two of the remaining trees towering over a barley crop in 2007, but sadly in the intervening years both trees have been lost.

North Wessex Downs near Ashmansworth
I spent much of the spring and early summer of 2010 working on a wildflower project, aiming to capture the beauty of native flowers in their landscape setting. Many days were spent scouting around to identify locations where the subject – and surrounding countryside – were impressive enough to warrant a further visit.

As would be expected, I found plenty of clover, but rarely growing in enough profusion to fill the foreground of a landscape photograph. However, an exception was a very memorable spot high on the North Wessex Downs near Ashmansworth. Here I found a broad spread of red clover dipping away to a wooded landscape below.

I wanted to show both the detail of the blooms and the countryside beyond, so I had to frame the scene from near-ground level with a wide-angle lens. This perspective gave the pinky-mauve blooms the prominence they needed while still keeping the distant landscape in focus.

Red clover near Ashmansworth

A sainfoin crop adding colour to the landscape near Popham

Sainfoin near Popham
Although I have often seen wild sainfoin growing in profusion on Salisbury Plain, I have yet to find it in any abundance in Hampshire. But although the wild variety remains elusive, I have noticed cultivated strains being grown as an occasional crop in some parts of the county, particularly in the north and west.

I was out before sunrise in June to capture an image of this sainfoin field near Popham. The small rosy-pink flowers glowed in the misty air, while the dark outline of a distant oak loomed in the background.

Landscape near Farley Mount

As the Clarendon Way meets the country lane near Farley Mount there is a marvellous view towards Great Up Somborne Wood – not a single building can be seen as the land rolls gently away to the north.

From this spot in early summer I've watched the wind waving over green barley in the near distance. By late summer the fields look very different and this photograph shows the view shortly after first light in August. There was an intense stillness on this morning, and wisps of mist hung on the landscape where the stubble fields were catching the early sun. For a short while the whole scene glowed with a pale orange hue, and I used a long lens to isolate lines of trees that were standing in dark outline against the misty air.

Great Up Somborne Wood from Farley Mount

Viper's bugloss in June

Martin Down

The most westerly point of Hampshire is also one of its most wild and beautiful places. The site of a National Nature Reserve, Martin Down must be one of the best examples of ancient chalk grassland in Britain. It sits on the edge of Cranborne Chase and is bordered by Dorset to the west and Wiltshire to the north.

My interest in the area, apart from the appeal of its open landscape, centres on its wildflowers which look their best in early summer. I always visit in the early morning for the best light and the calmest conditions, but it has to be said that the down looks equally impressive later in the day when the breeze picks up and starts to sway through the long grasses.

Foxgloves on the ridge

A veil of mist on Chilcomb Down

River Test at East Aston

Nestled away in the upper reaches of the Test Valley is a footpath which gives some splendid views of what is a very English river. The waters at this point have been swelled by the confluence with its first tributary – the Bourne – just half a mile upstream. The river then advances in a south-west arc before flowing on through Longparish and beyond.

From the hamlet of East Aston the path leads through a meadow to a wooden footbridge, and then follows the river for a short distance. I chose this location in a spell of fine weather in mid-September. As the sun slowly lifted I worked on a composition which used the sweeping diagonal of the bridge as its main element.

Sunrise by the footbridge at East Aston

A reed plume by the River Test

Houghton to King's Somborne

As the Clarendon Way crosses the Test Valley between Houghton and King's Somborne there are some marvellous views of the river and its surroundings. At the first bridge, in the shadow of towering poplar trees, the water runs shallow over a wide bed of flinty gravel. Further along, the track crosses another channel which is thick with vegetation and often full of wading cows in summer. At the third and final bridge the river flows deep and slow, with long strands of vibrant green weed waving gently in the current. The path then crosses the Test Way before climbing over the hill to King's Somborne.

Between the bridges the route is lined with flowers in spring and summer, and areas of reeds fill the marshy stretches. When I followed the path early on an August morning the dawn-lit landscape looked wonderful, but I was also attracted by the graceful arching shape of a reed plume hanging heavy with dew in the still air.

Itchen Stoke

Between Ovington and Itchen Stoke the river turns towards the north-west and separates into two channels. The divided waters then run parallel to one another, shaping an elongated island, before converging once again a short distance downstream. The area is grown thick with sedges, alder and sallow, and there may be no better place to admire this fine chalk stream than from the footpath which runs the length of the island.

I took this route one morning in September and watched a lone swan making its way slowly upriver. As it passed it was caught in a shaft of light breaking through the trees to the east.

A lone swan on the river at Itchen Stoke

King's Hat, New Forest

In some landscape photographs the sky is uneventful, or is even excluded altogether from the frame. But there are times when the sky is so dramatic that it dominates the scene, out-shining the landscape itself. I encountered this at King's Hat on the edge of Beaulieu Heath one August morning when the mix of light and cloud was unusually impressive.

I had chosen the location because an isolated moorland pine can be seen in profile, with nothing else intruding on the skyline. As dawn broke a thick mist was hanging on the landscape, shrouding the base of the tree and softening the rugged tufts of heather. Above, wisps of rosy cloud developed in the southern sky, becoming richer and more vibrant before finally fading in the sun's glare.

A flamboyant sky at King's Hat

Heather in bloom on Backley Plain

Backley Plain

The stretch of open country between Linwood and Burley in the New Forest can appear bleak and windswept, especially in winter. Its flat and featureless aspect is broken only by a scattering of Scots pines, many of them grown short and twisted from their struggle with the elements.

But in summer when the wide open heath is in bloom the place has an atmosphere of its own. I visited the area – known as Backley Plain – on a damp August morning, and found the moor flooded from the overnight downpours. There was no breath of wind as I wandered across the saturated landscape and came to a heather-flanked pool with a crisp reflection.

In September of the same year I returned to see how the landscape had changed. The pools were gone and the grass that had been submerged was rejuvenating, and although some sprigs of heather were still in flower, the heavy scent which hung on the moor a few weeks before was gone. What caught my interest on this occasion were the dewy webs which were draped on every gorse bush.

A dew-laden web on the moor in September

Heathland near Ipley

In late August before the sun was up I took a path across the moor near Ipley in the New Forest where, earlier in the summer, I had noticed an attractive cluster of pines set in a remote spot on the open landscape. The heath was now in its last flush of colour – a haze of pale mauve interspersed with ferns worn ragged by the season. Looking closer, I could see that the flowers were those of cross-leaved heath, and some already had the rusty-brown look of autumn.

Pockets of mist evaporated as dawn broke, and the pines began to catch the first light in their upper branches, while on a distant ridge the silver birch were already shining in full sun.

Scots pines and cross-leaved heath near Ipley

College Mead weir on the Itchen Navigation

Cascade near Brambridge

The Itchen is not a fast-flowing or noisy river, though it does have a number of weirs which cause the water to run in a brief torrent. The site of one of these is on the Itchen Navigation between Shawford and Brambridge, though it now appears to be disused and overgrown. Known as College Mead weir, it can be seen from a bridge on the Itchen Way, and in its eroded state it looks surprisingly graceful, resembling a natural waterfall rather than a man-made structure.

On my last visit I walked from Brambridge, following a charming riverside path which leads past deep beds of comfrey and gives wide views across the water to Twyford meadows. Looking slightly at odds with the surrounding landscape, the rocky cascade was just visible between the extending branches of sycamore.

Hornbeams in the mist at River Park

River Park, Winchester

Anyone walking the pathways of Winchester's River Park is likely to notice a row of hornbeam trees, though not for their spring catkins or their brief flash of autumn colour. Instead these trees can be admired simply for their shape, being of a variety (*carpinus betulus 'fastigiata'*) which grows in a tight, rounded form. These specimens have become quite extreme, with each one developing into a huge sphere supported by a comparatively narrow trunk.

They stand between a rugby pitch and a cricket field, and although I prefer a more rural setting for landscape photographs, I've been fascinated by these trees for years. They number ten in all, though a couple are much smaller, having been replaced some years ago. The crowns of the other seven are getting ever wider and look likely to merge together in time.

For this slightly abstract view – a simple study of their shape and form – I photographed the five roundest ones in a misty atmosphere in late summer.

Moon Daisies at Mottisfont

While there has been a general decline in wildflower populations in recent decades, the oxeye or moon daisy appears to be thriving – in Hampshire at least. Every year May and June are marked with a profusion of these pretty flowers, sprawling along roadsides and field margins in thick beds of white blooms which wave in the slightest breeze.

At Mottisfont the Test Way passes through a meadow which has a marvellous display of these flowers year after year. I set out very early to visit this location, aiming to capture the scene in the soft sidelight of dawn. With a distant oak on the horizon, I was able to fill the foreground with the flowers. The sky was not clear, but the sun found a gap in the clouds and the landscape was illuminated with a warm glow.

Later that year, on a foggy morning after the field had been mown, I found an isolated daisy which had survived. With my camera at ground level I took a close-up view of the flower head, with the same oak tree in the distance.

'Moon daisy meadow' – Mottisfont in June

The last of the moon daisies, in August

Wildflowers on Butser Hill

Butser Hill

The chalk grassland at Butser Hill on the South Downs is decorated with wild flowers in June, and when I came across a thick cluster of kidney vetch and red clover on the eastern slope I planned a return trip to see them at first light. The location had a dramatic perspective with the hillside dropping away steeply – soon disappearing to give a sweeping view of the landscape beyond.

On the morning I returned there was a light dew in the grass, and I stepped carefully between the crowded flowers to a position where the rising sun was just out of the frame.

Knapweed at Appleshaw

Throughout July and August the vivid purple flowers of knapweed emerge, scattered through Hampshire's chalky districts, especially along country lanes and on the margins of fields. They enjoy a sunny site and so are usually seen jostling with other wildflowers, or partly hidden by long summer grasses. But in some locations they can dominate a stretch of land, like this disused pasture near Appleshaw where I found them knee-deep and humming with bees.

Knapweed meadow near Appleshaw

Thistles near Weyhill

As a common weed of pastures and hedgerows thistles are easily overlooked, even though at close range their mauve blooms are very beautiful! In Hampshire they are as abundant as anywhere, and their presence can be traced in place-names across the county – I know of at least two farms (Thistle Ridge near Marwell and Thisteldown at Minstead) which have taken their name from the plant.

I once came across a cluster of spear thistles growing in a fallow field near Weyhill, looking particularly majestic among tall spires of weld. The colourful mass of flowers was waving in the wind, so I returned to photograph them early the following morning when the air was still.

Thistles among weld, Weyhill

Summer grasses near Swanmore

Swanmore

The small lane which winds its way east from Swanmore passes through some apple orchards before opening out onto an arable landscape. From this point the route is unfenced, and in summer the verges grow deep with wayside plants.

I stopped here in early June to take in the views and found myself admiring the grasses which were swaying elegantly in the morning breeze. Intent on photographing them, I decided to kneel down for a close-up view, using the tall stalks of grass as the main subject and a distant tree on the skyline as a backdrop.

Longwood Warren

There's an air of remoteness about the landscape at Longwood Warren. Positioned on the western rim of the South Downs, it's a place of vast fields with few trees or hedges, and the lack of prominent features means the views can be quite stark and empty-looking. But

A sea of barley at Longwood Warren

this simplicity draws more attention to the shape and form of the landscape itself, which has to be admired for its gently-rolling aspect. This photograph was taken shortly after first light in June.

Dame's Violets
Though not a native of Britain, dame's violets have become naturalised, and each year I come across them – in all their varieties – in Hampshire's hedgerows, usually in the north of the county. They are very fragrant, and when I came to photograph this cluster on a calm morning in June the air was sweet with their scent.

As it happens, these particular flowers were growing in Wiltshire, but the landscape beyond extends into Hampshire and hence I have included the image in this book. Having set out in the small hours for this location, I became concerned when dawn broke that the banks of low cloud would extend and smother the sunrise. But in time my worries faded as the sun began to filter through from the north-east, bringing out the vivid colour in the flowers. The cloud which had threatened to scupper the image drifted southwards giving an atmospheric look to the countryside beyond.

Dame's violets in the early morning light

Landscape in mauve – phacelia flowers at Fawley Down

Summer on Fawley Down
After some lengthy research I identified the attractive plants in this photograph as phacelia. I noticed the field from a distance, as a shimmer of mauve on the hillside by Fawley Down, and as the area doesn't seem right for lavender, I took it to be a strain of borage. But I was intrigued, so early the next day I took the footpath from Cheesefoot Head to investigate.

As I came to the site I could see that the plants resembled thistles in their structure, but that the colour didn't quite match. Looking more closely I found that the spiky appearance was misleading, as the flowers were in fact covered with delicate hairs, and the whole plant was soft to touch.

The swathe of pale mauve set the mood of the scene, and with the green landscape and pale wispy cloud beyond it made a pleasing image of an unusual crop.

Harvest Time at Droxford

As the Wayfarer's Walk approaches Droxford from the west it passes a place where five lanes meet, on the edge of Shepherd's Down. At this point the landscape has a gentle aspect, different to the steeply rolling downland seen at Beacon Hill to the north.

Straw bales in the fields above Droxford

The lane which leads east from the crossroads descends to Droxford, taking in a panoramic view of the Meon Valley from Corhampton to Soberton as it goes. Known as Sheep Pond Lane, the route is bordered by vast fields – one of which was scattered with straw bales when I took this photograph in mid-August.

Morning light at Amberwood

Amberwood in September

On a damp September morning I travelled to Eyeworth Pond in the New Forest, a small tree-lined reservoir near Fritham. This quiet water is covered with lily pads, although the lateness of the season had left the flowers faded and the leaves ragged.

But the light was good and there was no breath of wind, so I took a trail westwards past the lodge and soon came to the edge of Amberwood Inclosure. Here a mist was hanging in the moist woods and I followed the course of Latchmore Brook which winds its way among the trees. In time the first rays of sunlight began to pierce the canopy, stretching in radiant beams through the damp air to the forest floor.

Ober Water

Although the New Forest has no major rivers running through it, there are many woodland streams – slow flowing on beds of gravel – which add interest to the environment. One of these is Ober Water which rises below Backley Plain and flows east to join the Lymington River at Bolderford Bridge.

Trees crowd along its meandering course, some of them with inter-twining root systems that become exposed as the stream banks erode. Inevitably, as time passes some of the trees lean or topple across the water, creating a chaotic woody spectacle.

The mature Scots pine shown in this photograph is poised at an acute angle over the stream with its root plate partially raised, and it has been in this precarious position as long as I can remember.

Ober Water meandering its way through the New Forest

Telegraph Hill near Chilcomb

The sweeping fields and woody plantations at Cheesefoot Head mark the western extremes of the South Downs. Walkers leaving the downs this way make their last descent from Telegraph Hill before entering the tiny village of Chilcomb.

It was in this area that I first saw flax being grown on a large scale, when the land surrounding what is known as Velpin's Plantation was carpeted with delicate blue flowers. I returned at dawn the following day, but the colour was diminished and the fields were more green than blue. I looked carefully and realised that the flowers had closed up tightly overnight, and wouldn't open for some time. So on this occasion I had to abandon the golden light of morning, and return when the sun was higher in the sky.

Landscape in blue – flax fields by Telegraph Hill

A poppy-lined byway near Larkwhistle Farm

Poppies at South Wonston

The network of byways which weave through the landscape around South Wonston is often lined with poppies, growing along the un-sprayed margins of fields. I took this photograph near Larkwhistle Farm where poppies were crowding along both sides of the track, all facing east towards the morning sun.

Poppies at Danebury

On a clear day it must be possible to see a distance of 20 miles or more from the top of the ancient hill fort at Danebury near Stockbridge. A patchwork of fields extends in all directions and it was from this point in early June that I noticed a swathe of poppies to the south-east.

I later found the location to be a wheat field on the edge of a lane and I was able to wander along the side to a place where the poppies were thick. Seeing one tall flower which stood above the rest, I decided to take a close-up view to show it in detail.

A poppy in close-up at Danebury

Poppies near Faccombe on the North Wessex Downs

Poppy Crop at Farleigh Wallop

The arable landscape of Hampshire has traditionally been one of wheat, barley and oats, creating a patchwork of fields lined by hedges and broken here and there by woodlands. From spring to midsummer the land became an almost unbroken stretch of green. But in recent decades this uniformity has been disturbed as two relatively new crops – oilseed rape and opium poppies – have made their mark.

Opium poppies at Farleigh Wallop

As a photographer I prefer a gentle mix of greens to the dazzling blocks of yellow which oilseed rape brings. But the foreign poppies which have been widely planted in central Hampshire since the 1990s do have their merits. Their huge white blooms are flushed with pink or mauve, and even after flowering the unusual tint of their foliage leaves the field looking blue-green from a distance. This photograph was taken at Farleigh Wallop where I noticed scatterings of rape flowers growing among the poppy crop.

Hay Meadows at Mottisfont
Photographers have long cherished the quality of light around sunrise and sunset, calling it the 'golden hour', a time when the landscape is illuminated by a warming sidelight from the low sun. It's nature's way that dew and mist can also form at these times, and wind is often at its lightest. When these elements are brought together, and the location is a hay meadow in July, there is a picture in the making.

Daybreak in the hay meadows at Mottisfont

I arrived at this location near Mottisfont in the pre-dawn light and made my way through the field to a patch of tall meadow grasses. Aiming for a sense of depth, I set my tripod at knee-height to capture an image which showed the slender stalks of grass in front of the receding meadow.

Lavender Fields

Few people would associate sweeping fields of lavender with the Hampshire countryside, though such places do exist. At Oakley, and on a larger scale at Alton, lavender is grown on a commercial scale in neat, tight lines – reminiscent of landscapes in Provence.

For this photograph I was able to find a place where the banks of lavender receded towards the horizon, with no other landscape features beyond. The result is a slightly abstract view consisting almost entirely of lavender and sky.

Banks of lavender near Oakley

Mist among the trees in the Test Valley

Test Valley Between Mottisfont and Horsebridge

From Stonymarsh a small escarpment runs northwards, rising to a highpoint of nearly 300ft. The elevated position gives a striking glimpse of the Test Valley as it stretches north towards Horsebridge. This part of the valley, shrouded from the rising sun by the high land to the east, retains a morning mist long after it has vanished from the surrounding area.

I visited the location in mid-August and was intrigued by the variety of tree shapes – spreading crowns and narrow columns – which I saw rising above the mist.

Popham

Although not ancient, the lonely yew tree at Popham Beacons is probably older than most of the broadleaf trees in the area. It's an unusual sight, if not unique in Hampshire, to see a yew growing as a landmark tree in such an isolated location. Its dense dark foliage gives it a brooding aspect, but its position and its neatly rounded shape make it a worthy subject for a landscape photograph. On this occasion I waited until early evening when the colour of the light brought out the earthy tones of the late-September landscape.

A remote yew tree near Popham

Ashley Down
As the historic Clarendon Way leaves Winchester it soon meets open country, but not until it reaches Ashley Down does it really show its flair as a scenic route. At this point it descends through the rolling chalk landscape and meets a quiet lane – once a Roman

Ashley Down at first light in September

Road – before ascending once more to a ridge bound for King's Somborne in the west. This peaceful location is surely one of the quietest parts of the region, and captures the essence of rural Hampshire.

AUTUMN

Itchen Valley in Autumn

I've watched the displays of autumn colour in Hampshire for over thirty years, and without doubt one of the finest came in 2001. My notes from that period tell me that the weather was mild and sunny, but not exceptionally so. More significant were the calm conditions, there being almost no wind for much of November when leaf colours were forming.

In that year it seemed that every copse and thicket became yellow as the trees held on to their autumnal foliage. In time the displays became richer, and finally even the late-turning oaks added to the beauty. The images on these two pages were taken in the Itchen Valley in mid-November of that year.

Part of the River Itchen near Alresford

The majestic avenue of lime trees at Avington House

Ash Tree on the South Downs
On the South Downs near East Meon is a remote hilltop ash, standing proud in its exposed position. The setting is beautiful, but I have to marvel at the tree's resilience, and wonder how it came to survive to maturity in such an open and elevated spot. The answer may be simple, as the wood of ash is renowned for being both supple and strong – it is the very stuff that cartwheels were made of.

The elements have clearly forced it into a rounded habit, shorter and more stocky than ash trees found in valleys and woodlands. We can only hope that its sheer isolation helps to protect it from the ash die-back disease which is advancing across Britain.

Emerging from the mist – a solitary ash tree on the South Downs

Sheep in a riverside field between Avington and Itchen Stoke

The Itchen Way

A small lane runs east from Avington Park, leaving the avenue of mistletoe-clad lime trees behind and following the river upstream towards Itchen Stoke. Beyond Park Farm, at the point where the Itchen Way joins the lane there are some splendid views of the valley – on some mornings the course of the river can be traced by the clouds of mist seen rising from its water.

I took this way on a frosty morning in October and the landscape was pristeen in the early sunlight. A flock of sheep were happily grazing the frosty grass in a field dotted with willows, and the whole scene was back-lit by the morning sun.

Autumn at Ovington

It's no coincidence that Ovington appears several times in this book – it's a place I'm very fond of, and one which I'm sure is loved by many local people. I've seen it in all weathers, having visited probably every year since my childhood, and it's always pleasing to see how little it has changed.

I've made several autumn visits, but my favourite was on a cold November morning when a sharp frost had penetrated the valley. I sized up the views both up and down the river, and decided to crouch among the reeds and take a picture looking directly across the water, where the rays of the rising sun were catching the autumnal colours of the riverside trees. The scene had an appealing contrast – the frosty blue reeds in the foreground set against the warmer sun-lit yellows in the background.

I often think of autumn as my favourite time of year for landscape photography, but of all my images this may be the one that portrays the season at its best – with a flash of golden colour, a dusting of frost and a hint of mist all thrown together in one scene.

Frosted reeds and yellow leaves – autumn at Ovington

Pines in the mist at Ovington

Scots Pines at Ovington

This small stand of Scots pines can be seen in a field near Ovington. Wild and graceful, it seems that each tree has developed its own character – leaning, spreading, or twisting in sinuous forms. I believe they are all that remains of a longer line of trees which marked a field boundary. This photograph was taken in 1999, and on a recent visit I noticed that only five of the trees now remain.

Bramshaw Wood

As a landscape photographer I have a particular liking for the effects of mist and fog. In woodlands in particular, the grey-blue tones add an eerie atmosphere which can lift a scene out of the ordinary. The perspective feels different, too – foreground trees appearing more pronounced as those in the distance become hazy, or disappear altogether in the moisture-laden air.

Bramshaw Wood in the New Forest was steeped in mist when I captured this image in mid-October before the autumn had really taken hold. Just a few patches of colour were appearing around the edges of the wood and on the younger trees – it was to be another three weeks before the leaf colours peaked.

I chose a view at the edge of a glade where some beech trees stood in a semi-circle, their trunks grown thick with moss. On a low branch a spray of leaves was flushed with yellow, and they seemed to glow against the pale misty backdrop.

'Season of mist' – early autumn at Bramshaw Wood

Hatchet Pond

My ramblings in the New Forest have shown me that it's home to a multitude of moorland pools, although the great majority of these are very small and vanish quickly in dry spells. Of those that remain many go unnoticed, being shrouded by deep heather on all sides. But there are a few exceptions, and Hatchet Pond near Beaulieu is perhaps the most familiar.

I've known this crescent-shaped body of water since my childhood, and still make the occasional visit with my family. Much of the surrounding land is flat and featureless, but if the wind drops late in the day its dark peaty water reflects the evening sky, and a moment of drama arrives.

Before sundown at Hatchet Pond

Rockram Wood to Brockis Hill

For whatever reason, autumn comes late in some years – in 2005 I witnessed many large trees in the New Forest still showing their full seasonal colour right into December. In that year I spent much time in the woods south of Cadnam, an area of beech and oak stretching from Rockram Wood to Brockis Hill.

In many ways this is the New Forest at its finest, almost devoid of tracks, and with trees which become older and more impressive the deeper you go. Some have beautiful mossy roots, while others have low branches which wander gracefully above the forest floor.

A stand of beech at Brockis Hill, still holding their last leaves in early December

An elegant, arching beech near Cadnam

Woods at Nomansland

Local people have told me that this stand of beech trees at Nomansland in the New Forest is known to them as 'the dark woods'. This name probably stems from the fact that beech casts a heavier shade than any other broadleaf tree – and, indeed, on summer visits I've noticed how the dense leaf layer screens all but the odd shaft of light from the forest floor.

Sun-lit woods at Nomansland in autumn

But when autumn takes hold the canopy begins to thin out, and in fine weather the slanting sunlight is able to reach down to the thickening carpet of leaves. As a rule I prefer cloudy conditions for woodland photography because it avoids the intrusive shadows caused by bright sunlight. But on this occasion the stretching shadows were a strong element of the photograph, giving a dynamic edge to the woody vista.

Great Huntley Bank

A New Forest stream known as the Highland Water rises at Stoney Cross plain and then flows south-east to meet the Black Water at a place named Queen Bower. Rarely is it a straight-flowing water, instead it finds its way through the centre of the forest by meandering continuously, leaving small ox-bows in its wake.

One of its most attractive stretches is along Great Huntley Bank, where strips of yellow-brown shingle have accumulated on the inside of almost every turn. The surrounding woods are lush in spring when only the clusters of holly with their dark foliage break the curtain of pale green leaves. In autumn all is awash with the yellows and russets of beech and oak.

I visited the area on a bright November day and found this arching beech tree on a slope above the stream. It had developed an interesting one-sided shape, and its dark boughs stood out in silhouette among the golden leaves.

A beech by the Highland Water at Great Huntley Bank

Autumn ferns at Berry Wood

Berry Wood

Berry Wood lies north of Burley in one of the lesser-known parts of the New Forest. It's traversed by a path known as Sir Dudley's Ride – named in memory of Sir Dudley Forwood, Official Verderer of the forest from 1974-82. The wood is notable for its fine stands of beech, and I'm sure it's no coincidence that the plaque to Sir Dudley stands right next to one of the most inspiring – a circular group of trees under-laid with a mossy carpet.

With beech so prominent the woods look supreme in autumn, and the bracken ferns which cluster in the glades add to the effect, turning from butter yellow to a rich brown as the season advances.

Ironshill to Ladycross

Going east from Brockenhurst the lane crosses the Lymington River before weaving its way into the woods. It climbs gently up Ironshill and then straightens out as it approaches Ladycross. Along this stretch it broadens out and the verges widen, yet the woodland canopy reaches right across, as the arching limbs of beech and oak meet and intertwine above the road. The route resembles a woody tunnel, giving travellers a sheltered feeling as they pass through.

There are many fine wooded lanes in the New Forest, but this must be one of the most spectacular – especially in a calm autumn when the leaves are able to develop their full colour while still on the trees.

Sprays of autumn leaves on the approach to Ladycross

Dew-laden webs on the heath near Holbury Purlieu

Holbury Purlieu

A small grove of pines are perched on the heath near Holbury Purlieu, a stretch of moorland on the south-east rim of the New Forest. I noticed them while out walking and returned some months later to photograph them in the dawn light.

As the mist burned away I was aware of the beautiful scattering of tiny cobwebs which were suspended in the marsh grasses at my feet. When the sun gained height it brought out the colour in the landscape and also caught the highlights of the dew-laden webs. At this point it seemed that nature had brought everything together and the image was made – beauty on a small scale in the foreground, leading to a greater landscape beyond.

Longwood Estate

The footpath which leads past the majestic grounds of Longwood House continues southwards and gives access to two impressive tree-lined avenues. The first is of yew trees, set well back on grassy verges along the track which leads down to Longwood Dean. The trees are still young – my guess is they were planted in the early 1980s – but being the slowest-growing and longest-lived native tree, they will hopefully be admired for many generations.

The second avenue is one of horse chestnuts and skirts the edge of Downwards Plantation to the south-west. Shorter in length and much narrower, this avenue allows the trees to meet across the middle, and also follows a route with fine views across to Dur Wood.

But despite the grandeur of these two avenues, it was a more ordinary scene which caught my eye one foggy morning in autumn. At the entrance to a woody track-way there was an enchanting view into the misty plantation which was scattered with fallen maple leaves.

A leafy track-way at Longwood

A frosty morning on the hill above Tichborne

Tichborne

The small hill north of Tichborne has no name, although it does have a number of footpaths and a fine viewpoint. To the east are the headwaters of the Itchen, with Tichborne Park beyond, while to the south the church can be seen, perched above the village and nestled among the dark profiles of towering conifers.

I walked this way on a crisp morning in late autumn, when the muddy tracks were frozen hard. As the rising sun clipped the top of the hill, it brought out the rich golden colour of the maize which lined the field.

River Test at Longstock

A slow-flowing side-channel joins the Test at Longstock, and though it lacks the stature of the main river it has an attractive meandering course. It borders the lane for a short way, and on one autumn morning I took a photograph looking over the frosted reeds where the water was snaking its way between the sunlit trees. The scene had a rustic look about it, and the combination of light, colour and cloud forms was reminiscent of a painting.

Late autumn frost at Longstock

West Wood at Farley Mount Country Park

I've spent more time photographing landscapes in autumn than in any other season. Like others, I'm tempted to the woods to capture the flush of leaf colour – vivid in the sunlight, or softer in the mist. So it's surprising that one of my favourite autumn landscapes should lack any golden hues.

The wooded downland at Farley Mount has many deciduous stretches dominated by beech which look splendid in November, but on the morning I arrived it was the misty silhouettes of conifers which first caught my eye. I made my way along a small ridge above the woods to a place where I could see the lines of treetops folded one behind the other, separated by the layers of mist. This view gave my picture the sense of depth I was looking for.

Mist between the treetops at West Wood

Mist on the landscape at Riversdown

Riversdown

A mist which hangs in hollows long after sunrise creates an eerie contrast. In its blue-grey depths colours are muted and shapes are softened, while the landscape and trees rising above it are crisp and bright with sunlit colour.

This was the effect at Riversdown near Warnford when I photographed the scene in late November. A pool of mist filled the foreground, making focal points of the tree-lined ridges which were flecked with the last hues of autumn.

Beaulieu Mill Pond

The northern part of the Beaulieu River is quite a contrast with the southern section. This change occurs at Beaulieu village where the river becomes a tidal water – above this point it is confined to a narrow course, but then it suddenly broadens out into a wide tidal channel which shelves gently from one side to the other.

Reflections in the reed beds at Beaulieu

Above the sluice at Beaulieu Mill is a large arc-shaped pool which rises and falls as the flow of water is regulated, and many people stop to admire the view – especially when the water is high. Hidden among the reeds is Bramble Island, created with the spoil from the rebuilding of Palace House in the 1870s.

In autumn, as the deciduous trees change colour, the banks of reeds follow suit, forming a continuous golden ribbon along the eastern shoreline. When the air is still the whole scene is reflected in a colourful panorama.

Harewood Forest
The footpath which follows the eastern edge of Harewood Forest offers great visual contrast. To one side is the shady woodland habitat with its tangled mix of shapes and forms, while on the other the landscape is open, exposed and well-lit.

The mature beech trees which line the woods are able to spread their boughs freely towards the field, arching them gracefully over the path. Lower down, their smooth silvery trunks are illuminated by the slanting morning sunlight as it sweeps in from the east. This special place is worthy of a visit in any season, but looks particularly spectacular in autumn.

Autumn beauty at Harewood

The avenue at Bradley Hill in autumn

Beech-lined avenue at Bradley Hill
Above the hamlet of Dunley a small steep lane climbs up Bradley Hill – twisting as it goes – before finally opening out onto the undulating landscape of the North Wessex Downs. One of our lesser-known Areas of Outstanding Natural Beauty, the Downs extend westwards from here deep into Wiltshire. But anyone travelling this way in November is likely to pause for a while at Bradley Hill, where the towering beech trees which border the lane make a showpiece of autumn colour.

Dunley

It's common to see small groves of trees planted mid-field as shade for livestock, wildlife havens or simply as landmarks. But they are usually broadleaf varieties, like the oaks at Mottisfont or the beech at Tunworth Down. It's more unusual to see pines used like this, but at Dunley there are a number of them planted in two circular groups in a field to the east of the village. Regardless of their original purpose the trees now have great ornamental value, adding interest and character to the arable landscape.

Islands of pine in the fields at Dunley

WINTER

Beech tree in snow at Matterley Bowl

Matterley Bowl

Whether seen from the road or the South Downs Way, the Matterley Bowl at Cheesefoot Head is an impressive sight. A natural amphitheatre, I've come to know the area as a frost pocket, or a misty hollow which retains a pool of fog long after sunrise. Its position, opening to the north-west, means it is one of the last places in the district to catch the morning sun. This shapely beech tree, which stands isolated above the bowl, was photographed shortly after sunrise in mid-winter.

Deer on the downs at East Meon

South Downs at East Meon
From the Bronze Age barrows on top of Old Winchester Hill the South Downs Way follows a zigzag course eastwards to its next summit on Salt Hill. This is one of the highest points in the county, its crest marked with a triangulation pillar at 768 feet. From here the landscape plummets away to the east, giving some fine views onto the fields below.

In the deep snows of 2009 I made a special outing to this area to capture the downland scenery in its winter beauty. In particular I was keen to photograph a remote beech tree which stands prominent in the open landscape below Wether Down. I spent some time finding the best viewpoint and by chance noticed a small herd of deer at the base of the nearby Hyden Hill. They began to venture into the field and in time made their way to the beech tree in the centre.

I've never actively pursued wildlife photography, so it was only by good fortune that I was able to capture an image of this fine sight.

Tree-lined Track near Middleton

Going south-east from Andover Down, the route to Middleton is a quiet 2-mile run along a country lane, which passes through stretches of Harewood Forest. Midway the road opens out to fields, the woods become distant, and for a while a fine expanse of landscape can be enjoyed with neither hedges nor fences to obscure the view.

A little further on the lane crosses part of the dismantled Test Valley railway, the section that ran from Hurstbourne Priors to Longparish which was last used in 1956. The tracks were removed and this stretch has since been invaded by sycamores. From here a footpath leads to Forton, while in the other direction there is a glimpse of a farm track lined with small maples. This photograph shows these trees after a recent blizzard when banks of freezing fog swept across southern England.

Leafless maples along the farm track near Middleton

Landscape at Avington

From the small village of Avington a footpath leads southwards and follows the edge of an extensive field surrounded by woods. The area is frequented by deer and it's an idyllic location – the land dips gently towards the centre of the field and there are a few small islands of trees, mostly beech, ash and lime. This photograph was taken in December 2006 when a cold spell brought a blanket of hoar frost to southern England. It shows the view looking south-west across the field towards Beech Hill.

Statuesque trees at Avington in winter

Winter at the downland pool, east of Selborne

Downland at Selborne

Nestled in the downland near the site of Selborne Priory is a small oval pool, its edges lined with tufts of rushes. Above is Coombe Wood and running alongside is the Oakhanger Stream, a tiny watercourse which ultimately drains into the River Wey. The place has an air of remoteness, for although it is less than a mile from Selborne and between two footpaths, there are no unnatural sounds to be heard.

I came across the pool on a damp winter's day when exploring the Monks' Walk along the muddy track from Wick Hill. The scene was different when I returned on a cold clear morning, the sun was still low and casting a delicate side-light as I made my way through the frosty grass. I chose to photograph a view looking across the water where the profile of an oak was reflected.

Windmill Hill

The road which leads from Stockbridge to Winchester is a scenic one which climbs out of the Test Valley and within a mile reaches Stockbridge Down. The road then dips gently for a mile before rising once again as it approaches the beech plantation known as Crawley Forest which spreads across Windmill Hill.

Leaving the main road, a small lane heads north – a beautiful tree-lined route which eventually emerges from the woods on the brow of the hill, giving a view towards Chilbolton Down. The lane then continues, descending the hill and passing a gated track which leads west to Long Copse. This image shows the view from the gateway on a crisp January morning before the frost had melted.

Frosty trackway by Windmill Hill

Oaks by the drove road on Itchen Stoke Down

Itchen Stoke Down

The central chalkland of Hampshire has a network of historic tracks known as 'drove roads'. These were the routes used to move livestock between pastures or to market, and form part of the county's rural heritage. A number of these droves unite at Itchen Stoke Down, west of Old Alresford, and are used by walkers to access the local landscape.

The down itself reaches a highpoint of only 400ft, at a point marked by a triangulation pillar which stands by a now derelict wind pump. Though modest in height, the location has sufficient elevation to give spreading views of the county's heartland.

The field oaks in this image stand alongside the northern drove where it crosses the lane which traverses the down. Based on the girth of their trunks they are likely to date from the latter part of the nineteenth century.

Hartley Pond
The deserted medieval settlement of Hartley Mauditt lies 3 miles south-east of Alton, where a twelfth-century church stands beside a large pond. An atmospheric place, it was mentioned in the Domesday Book, and can be easily explored by a network of footpaths.

My interest centres on the pond, a spring-fed water lined with bulrushes. The surrounding trees are conspicuous for their winter colour, having bark and twigs that are shades of red and orange, tones which are enhanced by the warming glow of a setting sun.

I set out for this location on a clear winter's afternoon, hoping to photograph the pond in some late sunlight. When lining-up the view I positioned the water's edge across the middle of the frame, using it as a central axis to emphasize the top-to-bottom symmetry. It was calm, but not completely still, with a slight breath of wind taking the sharpness from the reflection. To my eye the scene is more akin to a French landscape than an English one.

Evening reflections on the pond at Hartley Mauditt

Janesmoor Pond

The shallow circle of water known as Janesmoor Pond could easily go unnoticed, being only a stone's throw wide and shrouded from the road by gorse bushes. It lies on the edge of Janesmoor Plain, a stretch of land as flat as a pancake between Fritham and Stoney Cross, and though easily missed by passers-by it is certainly popular with ducks and ponies.

But this unassuming water comes into its own at sunset when it mirrors the western sky, and so it's been my last port of call on a number of autumn days spent in the New Forest. That said, my favourite photograph of this place was actually taken on a murky winter's morning when grey-blue tones pervaded the landscape and the eerie-looking frameworks of trees were reflected in the cold water.

Midwinter mist – Janesmoor Pond at dawn

Milbarrow Down

There have been a number of 'big freeze' events in recent years, but for me the most memorable was in the early weeks of 2009, when it was reported that Britain experienced some of its heaviest snowfalls for nearly twenty years. The hoar frost reached right into the woods, and for several days every branch and twig was coated in snow.

This image, taken on 10 January that year, shows a beech tree in the freezing fog on Milbarrow Down near Beauworth. It looked supreme dressed in white, framed by the branches of another tree close by. But extreme weather has since taken its toll on this majestic tree, which has lost a number of limbs since the photograph was taken, and is now little more than a relic.

Dressed in white – snow in the trees on Milbarrow Down

Side-lit pines at Rhinefield

Rhinefield

Weaving its way through majestic redwoods and Douglas firs, the Rhinefield Ornamental Drive is perhaps the most renowned route in the New Forest. It extends for over a mile between Vinney Ridge and Poundhill, crossing the Black Water at an arched bridge where exotic-looking woodland ferns line the stream bank in summer.

On a winter's day when I was exploring this area there were frequent heavy downpours which made my work difficult. However, the quality of sunlight which emerges after rain can be first rate, and finally – late in the day – conditions settled and the rainclouds subsided. Venturing into the woodland I came to an area of tall pines by a grassy glade, their trunks gilded in the side-light, and standing in stark contrast against the shadowy trees behind. An after-effect of the rain was a fine mist which rose up from the damp forest, adding a powerful atmosphere as the sun continued to flood in.

Snowdrops at Northington

Aside from their obvious beauty, I've always valued snowdrops as a photographic subject for the natural contrast they provide. At a time when winter still prevails they emerge fresh and white against the muted backdrop of a dormant landscape. They appear in tight clusters in many of Hampshire's woodlands and hedges, and under beech trees they look particularly striking against the brown carpet of leaves.

I prefer to photograph them early in the season, before the flower heads open and the 'droplet' shape is lost. I found this colony in woods near Northington and used the trunk of an ancient beech to provide some structure to the image. The extending mossy roots lead the eye across the picture, separating foreground from background.

Wild snowdrops at Northington in February

Upper Test Valley

In spells of fine weather a morning mist fills the meadowland between Hurstbourne Priors and Longparish, slowly ebbing and flowing until finally evaporating in the sunlight.

I passed this way in late February, and from a gateway by the lane I was struck by the imposing outline of a solitary ash tree. I had noticed the tree some years before but had never seen it in its leafless form, with its branches tapering in all directions to finely-traced twigs. Although ash is perhaps not as elegant in profile as beech or sycamore, this mature specimen made a fine focal point in the misty setting of the valley floor.

Ash tree near Longparish

An oak in the landscape at Sparsholt

Field Oak at Sparsholt

On a cold winter's morning I took the byway which leads into the downland west of Sparsholt. The route gives sweeping views in all diretions, broken only by a couple of barns perched along the way. Perhaps the highlight of this walk is a single majestic oak which stands mid-field to the north, and this was the subject I had in mind as I made my way along the frosty path.

The tree has a beautiful rounded crown, but also has a slight lean. However, its tilting aspect is appealing, so I chose a position which shows the tree leaning towards the centre of the rolling landscape.

Waves of snow on Worthy Down

Worthy Down

Worthy Down lies just north of Winchester between Three Maids Hill and Larkwhistle Farm. It's the site of an ancient field system, and a pleasant stretch of country which borders onto two clumps of broadleaf woodland – Worthy Grove and Little Grove.

This view of the down shows it on a crisp, clear morning following an overnight blizzard. The sky was of the clearest blue and every twig was dusted white, but for me the most appealing feature was the wave-like shapes created by the snow which overlaid the clumps of grass.

The image was taken on 19 December 1999, providing a glimpse of what was to be Hampshire's last snowfall of the millennium.

Last light at Hurst Spit

Hurst Spit

The focus of this book has been the inland beauty of Hampshire, but as a closing image I've chosen a view of the sea. Stretching for over 60 miles (including the major inlets) between Highcliffe in the west and Chichester Harbour in the east, Hampshire's coast is mostly one of sand and shingle and, with the exception of Hordle Cliff, is gentle and low-lying.

On a falling tide in late November, when a heavy ceiling of cloud stretched along the south coast, I made my way over the shingle bank of Hurst Spit. From the top I noticed a thin line of clear sky above the horizon, far to the west of the Needles. With a promise of some late sunlight, I found a viewpoint among the rocks – massive lumps of dark larvikite brought in from Norway in 1996 to defend the coast.

As sunset arrived there was a brief flash of light as the sun shone like an orange beacon beneath the darkening cloud.